OXFORD

T0352833

Coventry Carol

Roderick Williams

MUSIC DEPARTMENT

OXFORD
UNIVERSITY PRESS

Coventry Carol

from the *Pageant of the
Shearmen and Tailors* (15th cent.)
arr. RODERICK WILLIAMS

Originally published in Bullard (ed.), *The Oxford Book of Flexible Carols* (ISBN 978–0–19–336462–2) in a version for flexible voices.

* The keyboard part may be omitted entirely or in part. Alternatively, the accompaniment may be played by two appropriate melody instruments (e.g. violin and cello).

Duration: 2 mins

X823 Coventry Carol (SATB) WILLIAMS

ISBN 978-0-19-355165-7

9 780193 551657